ENTERTAINERS

Picture research by Faith Perkins

Printed in Italy

Library of Congress Cataloging-in-Publication Data

Richardson, Wendy
    Entertainers: through the eyes of artists/ by Wendy and Jack
      Richardson.   p.   cm. – (The World of art)
    Reprint. Originally published: Houndmills, Basingstoke,
Hampshire: Macmillan, 1989.
    Summary: Presents paintings and prints by notable artists
expressing ideas about entertainment. Includes descriptive
material about each artist and the accompanying work.
    ISBN 0-516-09283-9
    1. Entertainers in art – Juvenile literature. 2. Art – Juvenile
literature.
[1. Entertainers in art. 2. Artists. 3. Art appreciation.]
I. Richardson, Jack, 1940-   . II. Title. III. Series: Richardson,
Wendy. World of art.
N8217.E55R54 1990
760′.0442–dc20   90-34278
                                              CIP
                                              AC

Photographic acknowledgments
The authors and publishers wish to acknowledge with thanks, the following photographic sources:

Cover: The Concert – National Gallery, London
London Philharmonic Orchestra Rehearsing II, 1982 –
© Patrick Procktor, The Redfern Gallery, London, 3
Beryl Cook – © Beryl Cook (Photograph Rogers, Coleridge and White Ltd), 6
The Concert – National Gallery, London, 9
The Flute Player – Nationalmuseum, Stockholm, 11
Picasso – Musée Picasso, Paris © DACS 1988
(Visual Arts Library), 12
Three Musicians – The Museum of Modern Art, New York,
Mrs Simon Guggenheim fund © DACS 1988, 13
Edward Burra, 14
Newport – Photograph courtesy of The Lefevre Gallery, London, 15
Braques – Collection Larens (Visual Arts Library), 16
Aria de Bach – Pompidou Center © ADAGP, Paris/DACS, London 1988 (Lauros – Giraudon), 17
Colin Lanceley, 18

Kindly Shoot the Piano Player – © Colin Lanceley, 19
Lowry – Salford Art Gallery and Museum (The Bridgeman Art Library), 20
The Bandstand, Peel Park, Salford – City of York Art Gallery (The Bridgeman Art Library), 20
Degas – The Metropolitan Museum of Art, New York. Bequest of Stephen C. Clark, 1960, 22
Dancers, Pink and Green – The Metropolitan Museum of Art, New York. Bequest of Mrs H. O. Havemeyer, 1929. The H. O. Havemeyer Collection, 23
The Dance (First Version) – The Museum of Modern Art, New York.
Gift of Nelson A. Rockefeller in honor of Alfred H. Barr, Jr.
© Succession Henri Matisse/DACS 1988, 25
Philip Evergood – Hirshhorn Museum and Sculpture Garden Smithsonian Institution. Gift of Joseph H. Hirshhorn, 1966, 26
The Dance Marathon – Archer M. Huntington Art Gallery, The University of Texas at Austin, lent by James and Mari Michiner, 27
Beryl Cook – © Beryl Cook (Photograph Rogers, Coleridge and White Ltd), 28
Come Dancing – © Beryl Cook (Photograph Rogers, Coleridge and White Ltd), 29
Toulouse-Lautrec – Musée des Augustines, Toulouse, 30
Poster for the Moulin Rouge – Private Collection (The Bridgeman Art Library), 31
Walter Sickert – National Portrait Gallery, London, 32
The Old Bedford, a Corner of the Gallery – Walker Art Gallery, Liverpool. The National Museums and Galleries of Merseyside, 33
Portrait of the Actors Sawamura Sojuro and Segawa Kikusaburo – The Victoria and Albert Museum, London, 35
John Singer Sargent – Tate Gallery, London, 36
Ellen Terry as Lady Macbeth – Tate Gallery, London, on loan to the National Portrait Gallery, 37
Paul Klee – Bildarchiv Felix Klee © COSMOPRESS, Geneva, DACS, London 1988, 38
The Actor's Mask/Schauspieler – Maske – The Museum of Modern Art, New York. The Sidney and Harriet Janis Collection © COSMOPRESS, Geneva, DACS, London 1988, 39
Andy Warhol – Tate Gallery, London © Copyright – The Estate of Andy Warhol/DACS 1988, 40
Marilyn – Tate Gallery, London © Copyright – The Estate of Andy Warhol/DACS 1988 (The Bridgeman Art Library), 41
Seurat – Philadelphia Institute of Art (Visual Art Library), 42
The Circus – Musée d'Orsay, Paris (Lauros – Giraudon), 43
Dame Laura Knight – (Camera Press), 44
Circus Girl – Standberg Cove Gallery, London (The Bridgeman Art Library), 45
Brueghel – (The Mansell Collection), 46
Children's Games – Kunsthistorisches Museum, Vienna (The Bridgeman Art Library), 47

Introduction

This is a book of pictures about people enjoying themselves. Some of the pictures are old, and some of them were painted quite recently. They come from all over the world. Some are prints but most of them are paintings. One or two are made from some rather unusual materials.

They look very different, and the purposes for which they were painted were different, but they have one thing in common. They were made by people who had been thinking about entertainment, and thought that the best way to share their ideas was through a picture. So this is a book for you to look at.

The pictures tell how the artists feel about the many ways in which people amuse themselves. Some show people being entertained. Some show the entertainers. Some are of famous stars, some are of ordinary people entertaining themselves. Whatever they are about, they may remind you of something you have seen or done or heard, or they may make you want to get up and do something yourself. You may find sadness in the pictures or you may want to join in a scene of joy. Take a careful look at the pictures and see if you feel the same way as any of these painters do about entertainment.

Contents

The Concert

Oil paint on wood 3' 1½" × 2' 5¾"
Lorenzo Costa

LIVED:
1495/6-1535

NATIONALITY:
Italian

TYPE OF WORK:
portraits, landscape paintings

Not much is known about the life of Lorenzo Costa. Even the date of his birth is in doubt. However, we do know that when he was a young man he joined a painters' workshop and traveled with them from his native town, Ferrara, Italy, to Bologna. He is known as one of a group who painted "in the style of Bologna." Costa became the court painter for the wealthy Gonzaga family who lived in Mantua. His paintings are elegant and graceful and reflect the life of the court around him. He was also a clever landscape painter and is noted for his delicate use of color.

Art as a sign of wealth and education

The world of art in Costa's time was quite different from today. Wealthy people employed artists to make pictures or sculptures not only because they wished to own an object of beauty, but also to make sure that their power and wealth would be seen by others. It was the time of the Renaissance, when there was a renewed interest in ancient Greece and Rome, and in the power of the Roman Empire. People were looking again at the works of art and architecture that these classical times had produced. Wealthy families were in competition with each other to be more knowledgeable and appreciative about art. They employed musicians and poets as well as visual artists, and they sometimes expected artists to design useful objects as well as work on their painting.

A new fashion

This painting, a close-up picture of musicians, was the first example of what was to become a fashionable arrangement in pictures. It is painted as if the musicians were on a balcony; one looks at us, the audience, one has his eyes cast down in concentration, and the third is far away in thought. They are caught in the very act of singing a note. Costa has painted them close together, so that they are united as one shape as well as in one song, and he has placed them simply against a dark background. The musicians may have been members of the wealthy court of Mantua.

The Flute Player

Oil on canvas 2' 4½" × 2'

Judith Leyster

LIVED:
1609-1660

NATIONALITY:
Dutch

TYPE OF WORK:
oil paintings, especially portraits

Judith Leyster was a well-known painter in her own life-time. She was the only female member of the painters' guild of Haarlem in what is now The Netherlands and she had pupils who learned their craft from her. She was a friend of, and may have worked with, Frans Hals, who painted the famous *Laughing Cavalier*.

Using the light

The little flute player here is a typical choice of subject for Leyster. She liked to paint single figures and she enjoyed the drama of lighting a painting so that there are strong areas of shadow and brightly lit areas. A light is shining on the boy's face. Where do you think it has come from? Is it a candle or is it a larger light than that? The violin on the wall behind the boy is also well lit. Is it daylight or nighttime? The young musician is listening intently. Is it his own tune that has his attention? Maybe there is someone else with him.

The painting is a simple one and yet we become involved in it and want to know more. Leyster has captured a moment in a child's life and we can share it.

Line and color

The picture is well balanced, the vertical lines of the chair and the pipe on the wall make a frame for the boy. The rungs of the chair and the line of the folds in the boy's coat lead the eye up toward his hands and then the flute connects the eye to the intent little face. The color range that Leyster has used is subtle and does not distract us in any way. The boy's red hat in such soft velvet frames his face and keeps our eye on it, but nothing startles us. It is a very affectionate portrait.

Leyster herself married a painter, Jan Molenaer, and had at least five children.

Nationalmuseum, Stockholm

Three Musicians

Paint and collage 6' 7¼" × 7' 3¾"

Pablo Picasso

LIVED:
1881-1973

NATIONALITY:
Spanish, lived much of his life in France

TYPE OF WORK:
paintings, drawings, sculptures, ceramics, prints

Gallatin Collection, Philadelphia Museum of Art © DACS 1988

Pablo Ruiz y Picasso was a brilliant draftsman and painter even as a child. By the time he was sixteen years old he had learned all that he could at the art schools in Spain. When he was nineteen he made his first visit to Paris. He settled there two years later, but returned to Spain frequently.

The tireless worker

Picasso was adventurous in his work and eager to explore new ideas. He gobbled up ideas from everywhere, seeing the world with a clear, fresh eye. He worked tirelessly all his life. When he died in 1973, aged ninety-two, he had made thousands of drawings and paintings. He had filled 175 notebooks with sketches, observations and ideas, and it was upon this collection of information that he built his most important works.

What can you see?

Would you know what this picture was about if you did not see the title? Picasso has put together a collection of shapes. They are not really the shapes that we might expect would make up three people. Yet we can see the people. (If you half screw your eyes up, you can see them more clearly.) Ask yourself these questions about the picture:

What instruments are being played?
What are the musicians wearing?
Which one has a mustache and which a beard?
Are they sitting or standing? What on or at?
Where are they?
Is there anything else in the picture?

You can probably answer the questions though you cannot see the objects as you see a photograph. Why do you think this is so? Would everyone give the same answers? Does it matter if we each see a different picture?

Picasso's work is as much about his feelings and his thoughts as it is about the way things looked. This painting is from the period of his work known as cubism, but during his long lifetime he painted in many different styles, some concerned with form and color, some "realistic," some very emotional. He has had an enormous influence on art in the twentieth century. He was still planning new pictures when he died.

Newport
Watercolor 2'7" × 4'4½"
Edward Burra

LIVED:
1905-1976

NATIONALITY:
British

TYPE OF WORK:
watercolor paintings, woodcut prints, book illustrations

Edward Burra painted this picture when he was near the end of his life, and it has in it all the strands that together give his work its distinctive qualities. He painted it after a visit to Newport, a shipping port in South Wales. He was attracted, as he had been in many towns all his life, to the docks and the people who work in them. We can see the dockyard scene in this painting, the ships, the derricks, the freight cars and the railroad tracks, and the throng of dockworkers on their way to or from work. At first they seem a ghostly, unreal crowd. They are translucent and we see through one to the other. The objects of the dockyard seem more real than the people until you look at every individual, and see that each one is different and special.

A collection of memories

Also in the picture are two guitar players. They have nothing to do with Newport. Burra saw their photographs in a pop music magazine. He liked them, so he put them in this painting. This was the way Burra always worked. He was a keen observer of life and would sit for many hours in cafés or bars, or outside in the street, watching people. He trained himself to have a very good visual memory and hardly ever made sketches, but held everything in his head. In his studio he would conjure up his memories. He mixed images from real life with images from magazines and films. His paintings are a record of his everyday memories arranged in an order that pleased him.

The sources of his style

Burra trained in drawing, illustration, and graphic design at Chelsea Polytechnic in London and then went off to see Europe. He also traveled in the United States. He was always attracted to the working areas of towns and cities like Newport, or Toulouse and Marseilles in France, and the Harlem district of New York City. In places like these, he developed his style of figure painting, making his people slightly larger than life, but expressing strongly what he felt about them. Like many people of his time he was a devoted film fan and collected film magazines with their glossy photographs of the stars. His pictures are a sort of twentieth-century fantasy, composed of very ordinary objects and moments and the make-believe world of the films.

Photograph courtesy of The Lefevre Gallery, London

Aria de Bach

Pencil and charcoal drawing with paper collage 2' 1/2" × 1' 6"

Georges Braque

Collection Laurens

LIVED:
1882-1963

NATIONALITY:
French

TYPE OF WORK:
oil paintings, collage, lithographs

Georges Braque was expected to become a house-painter and decorator like his father, but during his apprenticeship in Normandy, France, and then in Paris he took lessons at art school and finally his family agreed to let him train as an artist. However, when he enrolled at a college in Paris, he found the lessons very restricting. He decided to set up as a painter without any further training. In Paris, Braque met many artists, among them Pablo Picasso. Together they experimented with new ways of painting. Braque said that they were like two mountaineers roped together, looking to each other for support.

It was an exhibition of Braque's that gave the name to the sort of paintings that they were working on. A critic said, "M. Braque . . . reduces everything, landscapes and figures and houses, to geometrical patterns, to cubes." So their work became known as cubism.

Mixed materials

This painting shows some of the ideas and experiments that Braque and Picasso worked on together. It uses a mixture of materials. It is drawn in pencil, charcoal, and chalk. Mixing drawing materials was not unusual, but sticking bits of papers and other materials to a painting *was* new. It is called *collage*, which means "sticking" in French. In this picture, three rectangles are cut from wallpaper. The brown rectangle is woodgrained wallpaper, which was very fashionable at the time. Sometimes Braque painted wood grain, a technique he learned as a decorator. The lettering on the picture was also an experiment introduced by Braque. It tells us the name of the picture, *Aria de Bach*, as if it were on the cover of a sheet of music.

In praise of another art

Like Picasso's, Braque's pictures are about the things he thought and felt. This picture is about music, which cannot be seen at all. Bach is a composer best known for his sacred music, and particularly for his oratorios, which are stories from the scriptures set to music. Songs for solo singers in oratorios are called arias. Braque made several pictures on the theme of music. (Another of his works is called *Homage to Bach*.) Braque himself played the flute, for which Bach wrote several pieces of music.

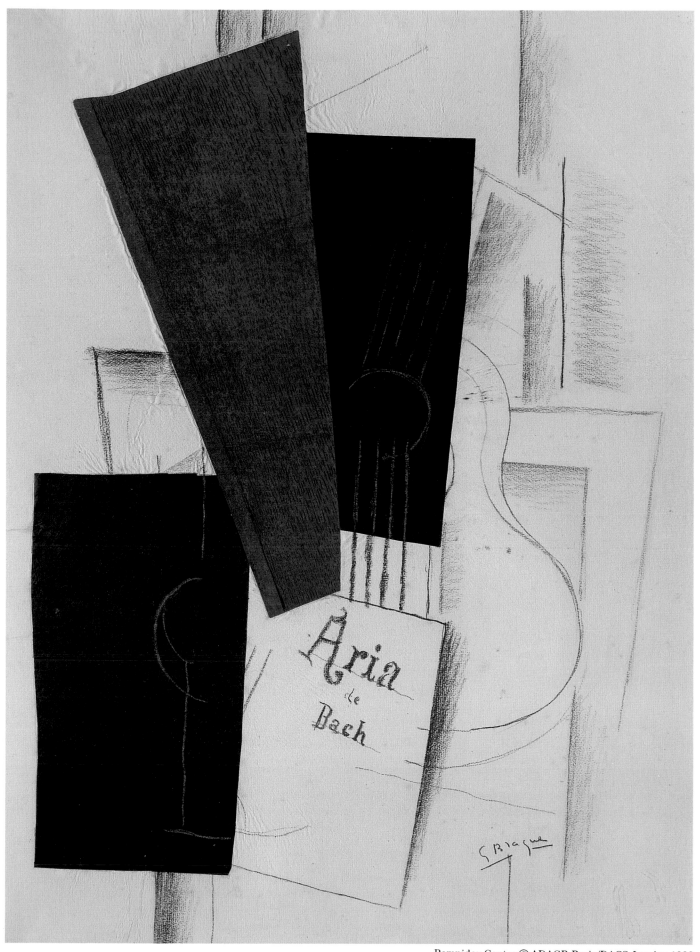

Kindly Shoot the Piano Player

Oils and enamels on mixed media construction 6' × 5'

Colin Lanceley

BORN:
1938

NATIONALITY:
New Zealander, lives in Australia

TYPE OF WORK:
paintings with collage, prints

Colin Lanceley was born in New Zealand but his family went to live in Sydney, Australia, when he was a baby. He grew up there, and became an apprentice in the printing industry at the age of sixteen. He enrolled for an Art Diploma course as a full-time student two years later. At college he made friends with two students and shared a house with them. They worked closely together, sometimes all working on one picture. They called themselves the Annandale imitation realists. They tried to make pictures that reflected modern Australian life.

An influence from Papua New Guinea

The three young men were interested in paintings and sculptures made by artists from Papua New Guinea. Lanceley was intrigued by the carved and painted masks and shields, which were like three-dimensional pictures. He enjoyed the way the artists had incorporated scrap materials, such as bottle caps, into their traditional pattern-making. The masks especially excited him. They were such strong images that they seemed to force you to look at them and react to them as faces. They had what Lanceley calls "a presence." He says that the way he knows that one of his pictures is finished is when he feels it has the same sort of "presence."

Working in collage

It was a combination of these ideas that Lanceley used when the Annandale group broke up. He started to work in collage. He said: "I felt that life could be seen as a collage, all human activity as collage." In this picture Lanceley's object is an old piano that he has taken apart and rearranged in a carved frame. He has also added a few more bits and pieces like the clock face. Can you see the influence of the masks and the carvings in this work? Does it intrigue you as the masks intrigued Lanceley?

Leaving Australia

Lanceley left Australia a few months after making this picture and lived in Europe, mainly in England, Spain, and France, for the next eighteen years. When he returned he had worked out how he could combine paintings and sculpture in pictures, and now he makes three-dimensional pictures of the Australian landscape.

The Bandstand, Peel Park, Salford

Oil on canvas 1'5" × 2'

L. S. Lowry

Salford Art Gallery and Museum

LIVED:
1887-1976

NATIONALITY:
British

TYPE OF WORK:
oil paintings, drawings

Lawrence Stephen Lowry was born in Manchester, England. The industrial scene was the landscape he knew and its workers were the people he grew up with. Lowry attended art school in Manchester until the family moved to nearby Salford. For many years he was a rent collector and spent his days in streets of little houses. He watched the people around him at work and at play.

A simple man

Lowry said of himself: "I am a simple man and I use simple materials: ivory, black, vermilion, Prussian blue, yellow ocher, flake white, and no medium. That's all I've ever used for my painting. I like oils. Watercolors I've used only occasionally. They don't really suit me: dry too quickly. They're not flexible enough. I like a medium you can work into over a period of time. That's about all there is to say about the way I work. I've done my best in my own way."

Lowry's "simple" painting was done with a variety of tools. He put the paint on thick with a brush or a palette knife. Then sometimes he would rub it away, or scratch through the surface with a nail. He usually painted on a white background, but the white would be varied. He sometimes made it gentle and creamy and sometimes sharp and bright.

Local entertainment

Lowry painted in and around the towns he knew well. He painted town scenes with an honest eye. He painted and drew this scene several times. He did not try to make it look beautiful. He shows the park, the little bit of countryside in town, surrounded by factories and billowing chimneys. The sky and the town meet in a smoky blur. There, dwarfed by the giant buildings, are the people, often called Lowry's "matchstick" people. They are thronging toward some fun. In the days before television, the band in the park was a very popular entertainment. Lowry was well aware of the hard life lived by many of the people he painted, but he was also aware that their lives were not all misery.

City of York Art Gallery

Dancers, Pink and Green

Oils on canvas 2'5¾" × 2'8½"

Hilaire-Germain-Edgar Degas

LIVED:
1834-1917

NATIONALITY:
French

TYPE OF WORK:
pastel drawings, oil paintings

The Metropolitan Museum of Art, New York. Bequest of Stephen C. Clark, 1960

Edgar Degas was a wealthy young man. He began to study law, but changed his mind and with his family's approval enrolled at a Paris academy to learn to paint.

Degas met and shared ideas with a group of young painters who became known as the impressionists. They tried to capture with paint a fleeting moment in time, and to paint what they saw rather than what they felt. Many impressionist paintings are of the natural world, and were painted out of doors in order to catch the exact effect of changing light. Degas was more interested in people and painted his pictures in his studio.

Long preparation

Degas prided himself on his drawing skills. He had an academic training and had spent many months in Italy studying the Old Masters. All his paintings began with sketches and studies from real-life observations. He would work on a painting for months, sometimes for years. "Nothing is less spontaneous than my art," he said.

Around 1870, Degas became interested in dancers and painted many pictures of them. He liked the way the dancers stood and moved, with a professional control achieved by long training. He preferred scenes that were undramatic and unemotional. He painted such scenes as if from a distance, as if he were hidden from the people he drew. His models are not posed for a painting. They look as if they are really at work.

Failing sight

This picture was made later in Degas' life when his eyesight was failing. He worked a great deal in pastels, gradually changing his style over the years. He began to work more quickly, leaving out a lot of detail, and instead creating areas of rich color. He had studied his dancers for years, and knew their gestures. These women are quite relaxed as they wait for their cue; one adjusts a strap, one tidies her hair, the central figure watches the shape she makes with her pointed foot, a fourth rests against a pillar.

Degas' sight finally failed and he turned to modeling sculptures, which he could do by touch. Perhaps his best known sculpture is of a little dancer.

The Metropolitan Museum of Art, New York. Bequest of Mrs H. O. Havemeyer, 1929. The H. O. Havemeyer Collection

The Dance (First Version)

Oil on canvas 7' 10½" × 12' 7½"
Henri Matisse

LIVED:
1869-1954

NATIONALITY:
French

TYPE OF WORK:
paintings and collage

Henri Matisse was born in a small town in northern France and began his working life as a lawyer's clerk. He took drawing lessons in the early morning before work began. When he was convalescing after an illness he obtained a paint box and said that he always remembered his discovery of painting as a kind of miracle. "When I started to paint I felt transported into a kind of paradise. In everyday life I was usually bored and vexed by the things that people were always telling me I must do. Starting to paint I felt gloriously free, quiet and alone."

Matisse discovers color

Matisse painted in a traditional style until, in the summer of 1895, he discovered the works of the impressionist painters. He was filled with enthusiasm for the way in which they used colors like rainbows. He began to be more adventurous in his own work and is sometimes referred to now as a master of color.

Energy through color and shape

In 1909 Matisse was asked to paint two large murals on the subjects of Dance and Music. He painted two versions of *Dance* on canvas. This painting is the first version, which is now in the Museum of Modern Art in New York. The second, which is much stronger in color, but very similar in design, is in The Hermitage Museum in Leningrad, Soviet Union. The dance that Matisse has painted is a traditional one from southern France called the *farondole*. It is danced to music with a strong and powerful rhythm. Matisse has used three equally strong colors to push against one another and move the dancers around in a circle. On the left the circle is broken and the dancers reach to rejoin it. Their outstretched arms suggest the speed of their movement. They do not quite succeed in reaching each other. We have to join the gap with our eyes and so we join in the dance.

Matisse has painted the dancers very simply as bold patterned shapes of flat color, with black outlines and features. They fill the canvas, indeed they overspill from it. Their dance is so full of energy that they seem to burst out of the canvas. The combination of equally balanced colors and strong shapes carefully placed on the canvas rectangle creates a very powerful picture.

The Museum of Modern Art, New York. Gift of Nelson A. Rockefeller in honour of Alfred H. Barr, Jr.

The Dance Marathon

Oils on canvas 5' × 3'4"

Philip Evergood

LIVED:
1901-1973

NATIONALITY:
American

TYPE OF WORK:
oil paintings, murals

Hirshhorn Museum and Sculpture Garden Smithsonian Institution. Gift of Joseph H. Hirshhorn, 1966

Philip Evergood, an American who lived and trained in England and in France for many years, had very different ideas about dance than either Degas or Matisse. Matisse painted dance as a symbol of human life and joy, while Degas was interested in the way people moved. Evergood was interested in the people themselves. He tried to paint in a way that would make people think. He was a social realist, and he thought that artists could help change the world for the better. He did not set out to make a thing of beauty but to try to tell a truth about life.

Dancing to eat

During the 1930s, when Evergood painted this picture, dance halls were popular places of entertainment for working people. Dance music was heard everywhere and radio and records were making tunes popular across the country. Every little town had a dance hall. The "thirties" were also a time of mass unemployment in North America and many people were unable to earn a living. One way to earn a little money was the Dance Marathon. Couples would start dancing and a prize, sometimes quite a large amount of money, would go to the couple who could stay on their feet the longest. People would pay to come and watch as one by one the dancers fell.

In this painting with its cartoon-like figures, the man on the left with a glass in his hand checks that the dancers are not asleep. Some dancers are collapsing. The sign on the wall tells us that this is the forty-ninth day of the event. A thousand-dollar bill is dangled above the competitors by a skeletal hand. A nurse in white stands ready in case of emergency. Important to the social message are the plump, bejeweled hands of the spectators that form the foreground of the picture.

With paintings like this, Evergood hoped to point out the desperate plight of some citizens, who would go to any lengths to earn money. He hoped to bring about a change in society, so that life would become better for poorer people.

Archer M. Huntington Art Gallery, The University of Texas at Austin, lent by James and Mari Michiner

Come Dancing
Oil on board 1'11" × 1'8"
Beryl Cook

BORN:
about 1928

NATIONALITY:
British

TYPE OF WORK:
paintings

© Beryl Cook (Photograph Rogers, Coleridge and White Ltd)

Beryl Cook started to paint when she was showing her son how to use his paint box. She found that she was enjoying painting more than he was! Once she started she could not stop. She paints on driftwood from the beach and on scraps from the local lumber yard. She paints people doing ordinary everyday things, in the streets and shops or at the park or pub. Some of the people are her friends, and some are people she sees passing by.

Beryl Cook has developed a style of her own that shows more than anything else how much she enjoys people and loves life, seeing the funny side in almost any situation. She is very observant of the way people stand and hold their hands. She says she is very fond of large hands. She also likes the way people wear their clothes, especially when they are dressed up for special occasions, as they are in this painting.

Larger than life
The same theme can inspire many different paintings. The timing and precision of the teams of formation dancers inspired Cook to paint this picture. Why do you think she presented the dancers and the judges as pigs? Where did that idea come from? Cook loves large people and often exaggerates size, but never means to be unkind. She laughs at herself in the same way, as you can see from her self-portrait. Do you think dancers would feel insulted by this picture?

Painting is hard work
Beryl Cook is a very popular and successful painter, but she finds it hard to get her pictures as she wants them. She has written of the disappointment that she often feels when paintings will not match up to her "beautiful vision." However, she says that if she keeps her pictures for a while she comes to accept them for what they are and feels glad that she was able to paint them at all. Then she finds that she misses them when they are sold!

© Beryl Cook (Photograph Rogers, Coleridge and White Ltd)

Poster for the Moulin Rouge

Lithograph 6′4¾″ × 4′

Henri de Toulouse-Lautrec

Musée des Augustines, Toulouse

LIVED:
1864-1901

NATIONALITY:
French

TYPE OF WORK:
drawings, paintings, lithographs, portraits, posters

Henri-Marie-Raymond de Toulouse-Lautrec-Monfa was born in Albi in southern France. His family were wealthy aristocrats. In two accidents when he was a teenager, Toulouse-Lautrec broke bones in both legs. The bones stopped growing, so that when he was an adult he was only 4½ feet tall. Unable to take part in many activities, Toulouse-Lautrec spent much of his time drawing, and in 1882 he went to Paris to take lessons in painting.

Finding a style

Toulouse-Lautrec was interested in the work of many of the painters whom he met in Paris, but he developed a distinct style of his own. His pictures are like drawings, with strong outlines and flat blocks of thin color. He also started to work in lithography – a type of printing.

Bold designs

Toulouse-Lautrec became very well known for the posters he designed for the theater. This one, designed for the *Moulin Rouge*, a nightclub in Paris, is probably the best known and was the first in his own style. It advertises the club, and the cancan dancer "La Goulue." Toulouse-Lautrec has drawn her dancing and showing her pantaloons and petticoats, for which the dance was famous. Her brilliant white and red costume emphasizes the energy of her dancing. She is the star of the show.

A little says a lot

The artist has made very few marks to outline the shapes, but the few lines give the swirling movement of the dancer's white frills. The boldness of the shapes and the astonishing color make this poster so eye-catching. The pieces fit like a complicated jigsaw puzzle. There is so little there, but it tells so much.

Because this picture was only a poster, it did not receive the care that would be given to a painting. You can see the marks where the poster has been folded, and Toulouse-Lautrec's carefully chosen and placed lettering has lost its top few inches. It was a large poster, almost two yards from top to bottom. It must have attracted a lot of attention on the streets of Paris.

Private Collection

The Old Bedford, a Corner of the Gallery

Oil on canvas 1′6″ × 1′11¾″

Walter Richard Sickert

National Portrait Gallery, London

LIVED:
1860-1942

NATIONALITY:
British

TYPE OF WORK:
oil paintings, engravings

Walter Richard Sickert spent three years as an actor before going to the Slade School of Art in London and beginning his training as a painter. This picture and others like it reflect this experience and his liking for theater buildings and theater audiences. After the Slade, he spent some time in Paris as a pupil of Degas, another painter who was interested in the theater and its people. Degas was to be Sickert's ideal painter throughout his life.

Sickert returned to London and became the leader of the group of young artists there. He was an English impressionist, trying to paint nature as he saw it, with no pretense. Sickert used quiet colors and carefully graded tones to achieve the effects he wanted. He spent a few years working in Dieppe in northern France and in Venice, Italy, then he came back to England. He taught at Westminster School of Art and also gave private lessons. One of his pupils was Winston Churchill who, as well as being a politician, was also a writer and a painter.

Dull or beautiful?

This is a picture of the corner of a music hall theater. Music halls were the theaters of the ordinary working people. They put on shows with dancers, singers, and comedians and the entertainment was lighthearted and fun. It was also cheap. The balcony, where we see this crowd, was the cheapest place and it was usually considered to be a bit "rough." Sickert has painted the audience absorbed by the show. The light from the stage catches the faces in a solemn moment. Perhaps they are listening to a sad song. The light also catches the gilded plasterwork that made the theaters seem luxurious and exciting. A large gilt-framed mirror reflects both audience and architecture and helps Sickert light a dark corner. This is just the sort of subject that he liked best. He chose to paint ordinary life, which some people called vulgar. He was not interested in "good taste" or what was considered to be refined and elegant. Sickert saw beauty where others saw dullness.

Walker Art Gallery, Liverpool. The National Museums and Galleries of Merseyside

Portrait of the Actors Sawamura Sojuro and Segawa Kikusaburo

Print from a woodcut block 1′2¾″ × 9¼″

Kunimasa

LIVED:
1773-1810

NATIONALITY:
Japanese

TYPE OF WORK:
woodcut prints, especially portraits of actors

The Kabuki style of theater was very popular in the cities of Japan in the eighteenth and nineteenth centuries. Kabuki is a type of drama with music and dancing that tells a story or legend. The tradition is said to have started nearly four hundred years ago, when Okumi, a young girl who looked after a holy place or shrine, began to tell stories through dance. She and her group of female dancers performed Japanese legends, based on very old writings.

Although women began this tradition, it was soon considered improper for them to watch the dances! It was not long before women were also banned from taking part. The actors shown in this print are both men. Acting was often a family occupation and some families of actors specialized in taking women's parts. These are two very famous actors. They would have been recognized by many people from their performances and from the prints.

Kabuki dramas sometimes lasted all day, with music and dancing between scenes. Heavy makeup and elaborate costumes helped create a magical atmosphere.

The theater was so popular that people wanted pictures to remind them of the plays just as we might keep photographs of actors or film stars nowadays. Some artists specialized in making prints of the actors. Kunimasa was well known for his particular bold style and for the larger-than-life-size heads that his portraits sometimes had.

A team effort

The artist made his drawing on a sheet of thin paper which was then stuck face-down on a piece of wood. Expert engravers cut the lines into the wood and the picture was then printed in black only. The artist colored the print by hand. More blocks were made, one for each of the colors to be used and then each block was printed on top of the other with great care being taken to ensure that the overprinting was exact.

Ellen Terry as Lady Macbeth

Oil on canvas 7' 3" × 3' 9"

John Singer Sargent

LIVED:
1856-1925

NATIONALITY:
American

TYPE OF WORK:
paintings, especially portraits

Tate Gallery, London

John Singer Sargent was an American but his life had an international flavor. He was once described as "an American, born in Italy, educated in France, who looks like a German, speaks like an Englishman, and paints like a Spaniard." The reference to Spanish painting comes from Sargent's admiration of the Old Masters, and in particular of the Spaniard, Velázquez.

A new "Old Master"

Sargent's mastery of paint and the elegance of his work brought him success in painting portraits of rich and famous people. His paintings reflect the wealth and glamour of a privileged class in society. He painted beautiful people wearing beautiful clothes in their beautiful surroundings.

Ellen Terry was the most successful actress of her time. Sargent has painted her playing Lady Macbeth, one of the most powerful roles in the plays of Shakespeare. Lady Macbeth is wicked and tragic. She makes speeches of great drama that give an actress opportunities to show off all her acting skill. It is a part that encompasses greed and power and, finally, sorrow and death.

A mixed reception

Sargent has not painted Lady Macbeth, but the actress playing the part. We see her stage makeup, with very red lips and black lines around her eyes. She wears a dramatic costume in vibrant gold and green and blue. Her hair falls in thick braids of glowing red, bound in gold right down to her knees. He paints her at the moment that she lifts the crown of Scotland to her head. Her posture is dramatic, her face a tragic picture.

Ellen Terry, who posed for the picture, loved this portrait. Some of the critics hated it because it exaggerated the ". . . sensational elements in her acting, and the coarseness of her surroundings . . . ." Sargent had painted Ellen Terry the actress and these critics wanted Lady Macbeth – the illusion, not the reality.

Do you think Sargent's painting has anything in common with Kunimasa's portraits of actors?

Tate Gallery, London, on loan to the National Portrait Gallery

The Actor's Mask/Schauspieler – Maske

Oil on canvas mounted on board 1' 2½" × 1' 1½"

Paul Klee

LIVED:
1879-1940

NATIONALITY:
Swiss

TYPE OF WORK:
drawings, paintings

Paul Klee was born in Switzerland and grew up in Bern but his parents were German. He was a very talented musician. At the age of twenty he was playing with the Bern Municipal Orchestra, and after his studies at art school he continued to play with them. In 1906 he married and moved to Munich, Germany. He began to meet other young painters but did not join any group style. All his life he worked as an individual.

Light and color

In 1914, with his friend August Macke, Klee traveled to Tunis. The clear light of North Africa had a great effect on him. He wrote in his diary, ". . . Color has taken hold of me: no longer do I have to chase after it. I know that it has hold of me forever. That is the significance of this blessed moment. Color and I are one. I am a painter . . . ."

A link with the ancient past?

All actors wear masks. Sometimes they are real masks, sometimes masks of makeup and sometimes masks that are their own features, hiding the actor and showing a different character. The mask is often used as a symbol to represent the theater and drama. In Greek theater, the actors used masks held in front of their faces. The masks had exaggerated expressions and told the audience that this was a tragic or a comic character. Klee could read ancient Greek and enjoyed studying the poetry and plays of the great Greek writers. Perhaps it was from this reading that he was inspired to make his picture.

An empty space

The mask shown here does not tell us much about any character. The face has become a sort of landscape with its bands of unnatural color. The eyes and mouth are like chasms, the nose is a steep hill. There is a strange smile stretching across the face, but the eyes have no pupils and no expression. The bright red hair is stiff and artificial. The whole mask has an emptiness about it. Is it waiting for the actor to bring it to life?

K Lee

Marilyn
Silk screen on paper 3' × 3'
Andy Warhol

LIVED:
1928-1987

NATIONALITY:
American

TYPE OF WORK:
paintings, screen prints,
photographs, films

Tate Gallery, London © Copyright – The Estate of Andy Warhol/DACS 1988

Andy Warhol was a picture maker of the Pop-art style, which often borrowed its images from film and television, comics, and advertisements. The style became popular in the 1960s. Warhol was first a successful commercial artist, in demand because of his technical abilities, drawing skills, and his efficiency. However, his ambition was to be recognized as a fine artist.

Everyday images
The first exhibitions of Warhol's work caused little interest, but a friend suggested that he try painting everyday, ordinary objects, such as dollar bills and cans of soup, objects so ordinary that no one looked at them properly. At first he painted them by hand, but soon began producing them on canvas using a silk screen. Warhol made many images of the same object. Sometimes he made them exactly alike, sometimes he changed the color. His new style attracted a great deal of attention.

His two best-known images are probably one of cans of Campbell's soup and this painting of Marilyn Monroe. Monroe was a film star of the 1950s. She was rich and famous, but her glamorous life was not happy. She died quite young. She seemed to many people to symbolize the glittery falseness of such fame.

Many from one
Warhol made several pictures of Monroe using this screen print. Sometimes he put several pictures together, using different colors for each print, and printed them next to each other in a grid on canvas. This print is a single image on paper. Do you think the portrait shows a happy person? What do you feel when you look at it?

Warhol made silk-screen prints of several pop stars. They were all done with the same crudeness of color and technique. This was deliberate. Warhol said he was aiming to paint like a machine. What do you think he meant?

The Circus

Oil on canvas 5' 10¾" × 4' 10¼"

Georges Seurat

Philadelphia Institute of Art

LIVED:
1859-1891

NATIONALITY:
French

TYPE OF WORK:
drawings, oil paintings

Georges Seurat developed a style of painting using tiny dots of colour which was known as pointillism or divisionism. He studied the scientific theory of color and of light and applied it to his painting. He made his pictures by putting very small dots of bright color one on top of another, so that the viewer's eye "mixed" the colors into more subtle shades. The result was a very clear and luminous effect.

Painting in this style took many hours of very careful work, but Seurat was a perfectionist. He often painted a border around his paintings in a darker tone, using his pointillist method, so that any shadows made by a frame would not unbalance the work. Sometimes he painted the frame as well in pointillist dots!

Formal designs

Seurat's interest in the effects of color grew partly from seeing the work of the impressionists, but unlike these painters, he was not interested in making his pictures seem to be natural happenings. He made very careful plans and organized all the parts of his pictures to work together in complex designs. In this picture of the circus, the stiff vertical and horizontal lines of the seats and the doorway and the upright posture of the audience contrast with the elegant curves of the circus acts. The central figures form a series of elegant, circular shapes. The clown in the foreground holds a curtain that leads our eye to the ringmaster, then through the yellow streamer we reach across to the equestrienne's outstretched hands, past the nose and hooves of the prancing horse and back to the red clown. Within this circle, a smaller one is composed of the acrobat, the horse, and the equestrienne who balances as light as air. As a result, the circus ring is full of movement. The red clown standing so boldly in the foreground cuts the arena into exciting shapes. The dominant colors here – red, yellow and white – are strengthened by the blue shadow.

Before he painted this picture of the circus, Seurat watched the show on many occasions. The picture was never finished, but it was near enough completed for Seurat to exhibit it just before he died. Seurat died very suddenly when he was only thirty-two years old.

Circus Girl
Watercolor on paper 1'4" × 2'
Laura Knight

(Camera Press)

LIVED:
1877-1970

NATIONALITY:
British

TYPE OF WORK:
paintings, drawings, etchings

Laura Knight's paintings were very popular before World War II. Her circus paintings were especially well liked. She loved the circus and circus people and spent whole seasons traveling with them. She painted the performances and the rehearsals, the preparation and the everyday work of the circus.

The traveling artist
Laura Knight trained at Nottingham School of Art in England and married a painter. She met and became a friend of A. J. Munnings, famed for his horse paintings, and he encouraged an interest in horses that Knight was to take into her circus work. She also painted gypsy horses and gypsy folk. Meeting them first at horse-race meetings, she became a friend and was invited to their camp to draw and paint there. It must have been a strange sight to see the traveling people with their caravans, and Laura Knight painting from the back of a borrowed Rolls Royce!

Knight was able to paint accurate sketches on her easel very quickly and would make many during a day's work. Then she would choose from among them and paint the final pictures from the sketches at home in her studio.

The tough side of circus life
This is one of Knight's sketches for a circus picture. Like the Seurat painting (p43) it is of an equestrienne, but Knight's aim is quite different from Seurat's. Both painters were fascinated by the circus, but while Seurat made an elegant pattern of lines and colors to show the magic of the performance, Knight is interested in the real life of the circus. Here she sketches a moment outside the tent. The performance is on. We see the lights of the ring through a tunnel of darkness. The next acts wait. This equestrienne is not yet part of the magic. She is the strong professional athlete. The second performer, holding the horse's head, has her coat on against the cold. She stands on straw in the mud of the entrance. This is the circus life "behind the scenes" that Knight came to know in her travels.

Standberg Cove Gallery, London

Children's Games

Paint on wood panel 3' 10½" × 5' 3½"

Pieter Brueghel

LIVED:
about 1525-1569

NATIONALITY:
Flemish

TYPE OF WORK:
paintings, engravings

The Mansell Collection

The details of Pieter Brueghel's early life are not known, but he was probably apprenticed to a painter who had studios in Brussels and Antwerp, Belgium. Brueghel married his master's daughter. He traveled to Italy in 1552 and 1553, visiting Naples and Rome. He died when he was about forty-four years old, and fifty of his paintings survive today.

A picture full of life

This picture is typical of Brueghel's crowded, bustling scenes. Some experts believe that he meant the work to be part of a set of pictures illustrating the stages of life, from birth to death, but this is the only known painting. It shows children of all ages, from toddlers to teenagers, playing all sorts of games. Many of these games we can recognize because children play in the same way today. There are about eighty different games altogether, including acrobatics, swinging on fences, hockey, leapfrog, swimming, hide-and-seek, climbing trees, fighting, chasing, blind man's buff, and dressing up. Many of the toys are recognizable too, such as hoops, spinning tops, and even a kind of balloon!

The children seem to be in charge of the town. They are swarming all over the place with hardly an adult in sight. It looks like a children's paradise.

A message for adults

Brueghel has not painted innocent and beautiful little children. If you look closely at their faces, many of them look very naughty and even ugly as they enjoy their games. The painting is not what it seems to be.

Although it is known as *Children's Games*, the painting is not really about children at all. Brueghel's paintings are usually very serious and tell a moral tale or give some warning about life. This one is no exception. It is probably meant to be a warning to adults who become so involved in everyday life that they forget that in God's eyes we are all children. The things that adults involve themselves in are as unimportant as games. God is in charge and people must remember that.

Brueghel had two sons of his own and must have watched them at play. He used all his skills in observing life around him in this complicated picture.

Some Ideas

For lovers of entertainment

You may have read this book because you enjoy being entertained. Perhaps you enjoy watching the circus or going to the theater or cinema. Perhaps you enjoy entertaining others and are training to be a dancer or a musician. If so, you might try drawing what you see or do as a way of understanding it better. Remember Degas and Seurat, who spent so much time simply watching people? Looking with a painter's eyes could help you to find out much more about your favorite entertainment.

For picture lovers

You may have read this book because you like looking at pictures. If so, perhaps you would like to see the original works. Remember the effect on Matisse of seeing the impressionists' works? A list at the front of the book tells you where to find those paintings that are on view to the public. They are in galleries around the world so you will not be able to see them all. However, your nearest gallery may have other works by the artists you like.

For those who want to be artists

You may have read this book because you like to draw or paint. If so, perhaps the book has helped you to discover some of the secrets of picture-making. All the work that is in the book is the result of hard thinking, lots of practice and, above all, very careful looking. Remember how Laura Knight traveled with the circus? Perhaps you could start a notebook or sketchbook when you next visit the theater, or watch your friends rehearsing. You will soon collect the information that will help you to make your ideas come alive.